This edition published by Mallard Press,
an imprint of BDD Promotional Book Company, Inc.,
666 Fifth Avenue, New York 10103.
Mallard Press and its accompanying design and logo
are trademarks of BDD Promotional Book Company, Inc.
Copyright © 1990 Victoria House Publishing Ltd.
Printed in Great Britain.

THE AMAZING BOOK OF FIRSTS

GREAT IDEAS

Written by David Smith & Sue Cassin

Illustrated by Kim Blundell

MALLARD
PRESS

CONTENTS

HOME ENTERTAINMENT MACHINES

T.V. BRIBE—In 1926 a Scotsman, John Logie Baird, gave the first public demonstration of television in his workroom in London. The first person to be seen on television was a 15-year-old boy named William Taynton, who had to be bribed with money to appear.

RADIO BROADCASTING—The first regular radio broadcasting was begun in 1920 by Westinghouse's Station KDKA in Pittsburgh.

In 1954 the first transistor was developed by Regency Electronics of Indianapolis. It weighed about three quarters of a pound.

VIDEO VENTURE—The first video cassette recorder for home use was the Philips 1500, first shown at an exhibition in London in 1971. In 1975 two Japanese companies (Sony and JVC) launched their own models—"Betamax" and "Video Home System," respectively.

In 1988 Sony brought out the first personal video. Pre-recorded films in color can now be watched anywhere!

FAVORITE MUSIC—In 1935 AEG of West Germany produced the first modern tape recorder, but in 1963 Philips of Holland introduced the cassette recorder. This used a more practical, small cassette instead of reels of tape.

In 1979 people were able to walk and travel while listening to their favorite music through headphones when Sony brought out a personal stereo tape recorder called the "Walkman."

RECORD REVOLUTION—The first phonograph records were invented in 1888 by E. Berliner of Germany, but the first long-playing records were developed in 1948 by Dr. Peter Goldwark and a research team at CBS. These records are the ones we use today that revolve at 33.3 rpm. The "singles" records were brought out shortly after this and revolve at 45 rpm.

The compact disc audio system was introduced in 1980 by Sony and Philips of Holland.

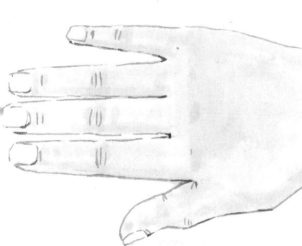

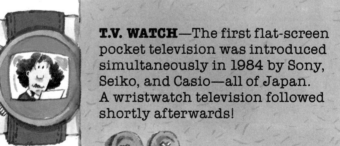

T.V. WATCH—The first flat-screen pocket television was introduced simultaneously in 1984 by Sony, Seiko, and Casio—all of Japan. A wristwatch television followed shortly afterwards!

VIDEO GAME SUCCESS—In 1972 Noland Bushnel, a 28-year-old, invented the first video game. He called it "Pong." The game was so successful that it enabled him to form his own company, "Atari." By 1975 Atari was mass producing various games for eager buyers.

INDOOR GAMES AND PASTIMES

WAR GAME—Chess is derived from *chaturanga*, an Indian war game, which dates from about AD 500, but the game didn't reach Europe until the 10th century. The game of chess may actually be much older, because two ivory chessmen, dating from AD 200, were found in Russia in 1972.

BILLIARDS KING—The first known game of billiards was played in France in 1429. King Louis XI, who ruled France from 1461 to 1483, was the first king to have his own billiards table!

SCRABBLE SALES—It took Alfred Butts, an architect from Connecticut, 15 years to develop the game of Scrabble. In 1946 he began making 200 sets per week at his home because game companies thought that Scrabble was too dull to sell.

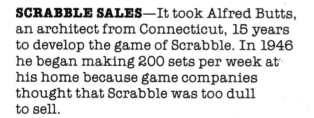

ARMY ACTIVITY—Snooker was invented in 1875 by British army officers serving in India. They were bored with billiards so they invented another game. Its name was taken from the word "snookers" referring to 1st year cadets at the Royal Military Academy, England.

PILGRIMS' PASTIME—It is said that the game of darts was played on the *Mayflower* by the Pilgrims sailing to America in 1620. The modern game dates from about 1896 when Brian Gamlin of Bury, England, invented the way the numbers are arranged on the board.

EGYPTIAN ENTERTAINMENT—Checkers has earlier beginnings than chess. It is known to have been played by the Egyptians as far back as 1000 BC.

TRIVIAL TRIUMPH—Trivial Pursuit was first launched in 1981. It was the idea of three Canadians—John and Chris Haney, and Scott Abbott.

CROSSWORD FIRST—The first crossword puzzle was compiled by Englishman Arthur Wynne and appeared in the New York *World* on December 21, 1913.

BEST SELLER—Monopoly was invented in the 1930s by an out-of-work heating engineer, Charles Darrow. It has since grown to become the most successful of board games—by 1988 more than 85 million sets had been sold worldwide!

JIGSAW MAPS—The first jigsaw puzzle was made in 1793 by a London engraver and cartographer, John Spilsbury. He started by pasting his maps to thick wooden blocks which he cut into pieces. When all the pieces were put together, they made up a map.

TOYS

TALKING DOLL—The first talking doll was made in 1823 by a German, Johann Maelzel. It said two words—''Mama'' and ''Papa.''

DOLLS' HOUSE BUILDERS—The first dolls' house was made by craftsmen in 1558 especially for the daughter of Duke Albrecht V of Bavaria.

LEAD LIFE GUARDS—The first model soldiers made of hollow-cast lead were a ''Life Guards'' set, produced by Britain's of Great Britain in 1893. The first plastic model soldiers were United States infantrymen. They were marketed by Betch Toys, New Jersey, in 1938.

LEGO LAUNCH—Lego was invented by Godtfred Kirk Christiansen in 1955. He used interlocking plastic toy bricks as developed with his father, Ole Kirk Christiansen, a Danish carpenter. *Leg godt* is Danish for ''play well'' and *lego* is Latin for ''put together.''

ROLLER SKATE CRASH

ROLLER SKATE CRASH—Roller skates were invented in 1760 by Joseph Merlin from Huy, Belgium. He was a violinist and wore his 2-wheeled skates at a masquerade ball in London. He skated into the ballroom playing his violin, but unfortunately he smashed a valuable mirror and wounded himself badly!

The first 4-wheeled roller skates were made in 1863 by J.L. Plimton of New York.

SKATEBOARD SENSATION

SKATEBOARD SENSATION—Skateboards were first used in California in 1966. They were improved in 1973 by using urethane plastic wheels. This was the idea of Frank Nasworthy, also from California.

CLOCKWORK TRAIN

CLOCKWORK TRAIN—In 1856 George Browne, a watchmaker from Connecticut, made the first clockwork train.

The first model train set with complete track layout also worked by clockwork. It was made in 1891 by Märklin Brothers of Göppingen, West Germany.

TOY ELEPHANT

TOY ELEPHANT—The first soft toy was a felt elephant made by Margaret Steiff from Giengen, West Germany, in 1880.

CANDY STORE INVENTION

CANDY STORE INVENTION—The teddy bear was first produced by chance by two people in the same year—1902. They were Morris Mitchom, a Russian immigrant, who made the teddy in his candy store in Brooklyn, and Richard Steiff from Giengen, West Germany. Mitchom is believed to have received permission from the U.S. president at that time, Teddy Roosevelt, to use "Teddy" in front of "bear."

FURNISHINGS

TIP-UP BED—Couch-like beds existed in Egypt as early as 2500 BC. The ancient Greeks and Romans used them to recline on while eating their meals and also to sleep on at night. Until the 17th century, beds were only used and owned by the wealthy and powerful.

In 1850 a bizarre "alarum bedstead" was invented in Great Britain. One of its features included an alarm clock on the headboard. When the bell finished ringing, the front legs of the bed gently folded and the person in bed was tipped onto his or her feet!

CARPET COMFORT—The first carpets were hand-knotted and made in Iran or China about 600 BC. Carpets were first woven on looms in the seventeenth century in France.

VENETIAN IDEA—In 1769 Edward Bevan of England devised Venetian blinds (window coverings made of thin slats that can be raised or lowered to allow light or air into a room). Bevan called them "Venetian blinds" because he first thought of the idea when he was in Venice.

WALLPAPER DISCOVERY—The first known wallpaper was discovered at Christ's College in Cambridge, England, during the course of rebuilding in 1911. The wallpaper itself is believed to date from 1509. It was made of small sheets, printed with floral patterns from a wood block, and was made by Hugo Goes of York, England.

ALARMING TEA-MAKER—
The automatic tea-maker was invented in 1902 by Frank Clarke, a gunsmith from Birmingham, England. The machine was set off by an alarm clock that worked levers and springs to strike a match and light a gas stove. It would then boil a small kettle of water, tip it up when ready to pour into the teapot, and strike the alarm bell!

CEREMONIAL CHAIRS—
Seats with backs used to be very rare. The first high-backed chairs were used in ancient Egypt for special ceremonies.

PLANTS' PARADISE—
In 1716 Martin Triewald, a Swedish engineer, installed the first hot water heating system to warm a greenhouse in England.

CLOCKWORK CRIB—In
1861 a clockwork cradle-rocker was invented, but was never heard of again!

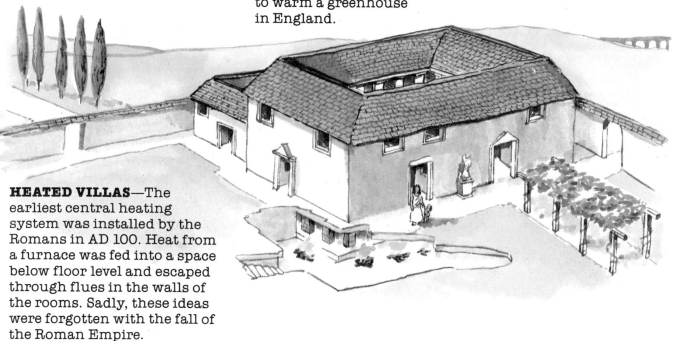

HEATED VILLAS—The
earliest central heating system was installed by the Romans in AD 100. Heat from a furnace was fed into a space below floor level and escaped through flues in the walls of the rooms. Sadly, these ideas were forgotten with the fall of the Roman Empire.

IN THE KITCHEN

CLEAN CLOTHES—The first electric washing machine was invented in 1906 by Alva J. Fisher of Chicago. It was sold to the public in 1910 as the "Thor" machine.

The first electric-powered wash and spin dry machine appeared in 1924, and was devised by Savage Arms Corporation of New York.

IRON INVENTION—Henry Seeley of New York invented the first electric flat iron in 1882. The steam iron appeared in 1938 and was the idea of Edmund Schreyer.

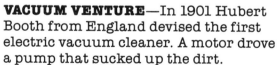

VACUUM VENTURE—In 1901 Hubert Booth from England devised the first electric vacuum cleaner. A motor drove a pump that sucked up the dirt.

The first upright vacuum cleaner with a dustbag attached was invented in 1907 by J. Murray Spangler, a janitor working in a department store in Ohio.

TOAST TIMER—The pop-up toaster was created in 1927 by Charles Strite of Minnesota. It had heating elements on both sides and a special clockwork timer that turned off the electric current.

PAN PROGRESS—The non-stick frying pan was the idea of Mark Grégoire of France. In 1958 he developed a pan coated with special plastic that is unaffected by hot or cold temperatures and is very slippery.

WONDER MACHINE—The first electric food processor was devised in 1936 by the Sunbeam Corporation. It had attachments to peel, slice, and liquidize fruit and vegetables.

FIRST KETTLE—Bill Russell and Peter Hobbs of England invented the first automatic electric kettle in 1955. When the boiling point was reached, the hot steam cut off the power.

STEAM ENGINE DISHWASHER—In 1889, after 10 years of development, an automatic dishwasher was produced for sale by Mrs. W.A. Cockram of Indiana.

The larger models were often used in hotels and could wash, scald, rinse, and dry up to 240 dishes of all shapes and sizes in just 2 minutes.

OVEN INVENTION—The first electric oven was installed in the Hotel Bernina in Samaden, Switzerland, in 1889. The electric power supply came from a generator driven by a nearby waterfall!

FRIDGE FACT—The first refrigerator for household use was made in 1913 in Chicago. It had a wooden cabinet on the bottom and a refrigerating unit on top.

IN THE BATHROOM

BATHING DUKE—The first person to have the luxury of hot and cold running water in the bathroom was the Duke of Devonshire at his home in Chatsworth, England, in 1700.

One of the earliest showers was also installed at Chatsworth in the 1840s. Water from a basin was pumped up by hand through pipes into the showerhead.

The first royal bathtub dating from 1700 BC was found in a queen's bathroom at the Palace of King Minos in Knossos, Crete.

MIRACLE TOOTHBRUSH—A Chinese encyclopedia published in the 17th century claims that the toothbrush was first invented in China in 1498.

The first modern-type toothbrush was made by a London tanner, William Addis, in 1780. Addis toothbrushes are still used today.

In 1885, a Dr. Scott from the United States devised the first electric toothbrush. In 1938 the first nylon bristle toothbrush—Dr. West's miracle tuft toothbrush—was marketed.

SEE-THROUGH SOAP—The earliest known recipe for soap comes from Mesopotamia and dates from 3000 BC. In 1798 Andrew Pears, an English hairdresser working in London, made the first transparent soap. It was not, however, until 1829 that the first wrapped-up soap—James Atkinson's "Old Brown London Soap"—was for sale.

RAZOR RECORD—The first double-edged safety razor was patented in the United States in 1901 by King Camp Gillette. Within one year a total of 90,000 Americans were using this razor and used up nearly 12½ million disposable razor blades! In 1931 the first electric razor was manufactured in Connecticut by Colonel Jacob Schick.

SPONGE SUCCESS—Natural sponges were used by the Egyptians. They used to soak them in honey and give them to their babies as pacifiers. In 1931 the first artificial sponge was invented by Novacel of France.

EVERYDAY ITEMS

LIGHT SUCCESS—Thomas Edison invented the electric light bulb in 1879. The bulb provided 13½ hours of light, enough for a long winter's evening.

AEROSOL IDEA—In 1926 Erik Rotheim of Norway found a method of spraying products such as hair spray, perfume, and paint from a can. It was not until 1941 that two Americans, L.D. Goodhue and W.N. Sullivan, developed this idea commercially when they sold the first aerosol—an insect-repellent spray.

SCISSORS STORY—Bronze scissors were in use in Asia and Europe as early as 1000 BC. Mass production began in 1761 and was started by Robert Hinchcliffe of Sheffield. The scissors were made of cast steel.

ZIP HITCH—The first zipper-type fastener was devised in 1891 by Whitcomb Judson from Chicago, and was very unreliable! In 1906 Gideon Sundback, a Swedish engineer, produced a fastener using interlocking metal teeth that were drawn together by a slide. This zipper was much more reliable, and the design is still used today.

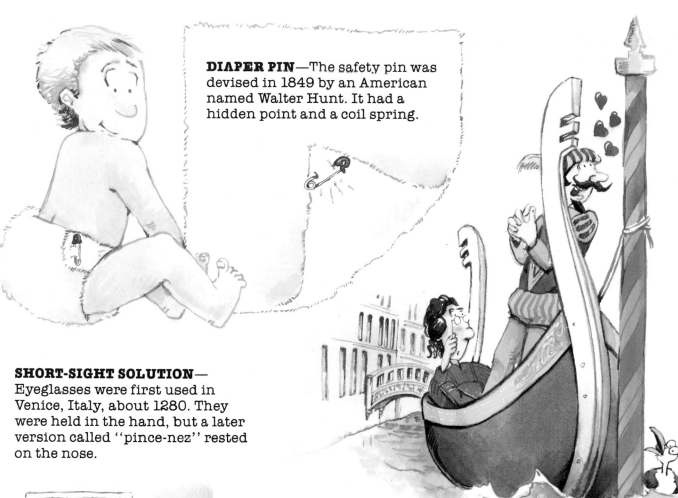

DIAPER PIN—The safety pin was devised in 1849 by an American named Walter Hunt. It had a hidden point and a coil spring.

SHORT-SIGHT SOLUTION—Eyeglasses were first used in Venice, Italy, about 1280. They were held in the hand, but a later version called "pince-nez" rested on the nose.

POLICE TRASH CAN—A Paris police chief, Eugène Poubelle, was very unhappy about the amount of waste paper scattered around the offices of the police station. In 1883 he invented the first trash can— a galvanized iron portable container. He had several of these installed to make the offices tidier.

WATERPROOF WONDER—Umbrellas were symbols of rank in China around 10 BC. The frames were made of either cane or sandalwood with a covering of leaves or feathers.

The first recorded waterproof umbrellas were listed in a 1637 inventory of King Louis XIII of France. He had three umbrellas made of oiled cloth trimmed underneath with gold and silver lace.

MORE EVERYDAY ITEMS

TREE DECORATIONS—In 1605 an unidentified visitor to France wrote that "for Christmas they have fir trees in their room, and decorated with paper roses, apples, sugar, gold, and wafers."

STICKY STUFF—Adhesive tape was invented in 1929 by Richard Drew of the 3M Company in Minnesota.

In 1934 James Chalmers of Scotland made the first adhesive postage stamps.

NON-BLOT PEN—The ballpoint pen was devised by a Hungarian hypnotist, sculptor, and journalist named Lazlo Biro. He had worked for years to make a pen that would not blot. Finally in 1945 his pen was produced by Eterpen Company of Buenos Aires, Argentina.

CHRISTMAS CARD CRAZE—The first Christmas card was designed in 1843 by John Calcott Horsley of Great Britain. Copies of it were sent by Sir Henry Cole to his friends. However, sending Christmas cards did not really become popular until 1862.

FIRST FLASHLIGHTS—The first electric flashlight was square in shape and was made by the British Electric Lamp Company in 1891. Sixty examples of this model were used by ticket inspectors of the Bristol Omnibus Company in 1892.

The Electric and Novelty Company of New York, (later known as the Ever Ready Company), brought out the first tubular electric flashlight in 1898.

FIRST ERASER—Mr. Nairne, a mathematical instrument maker from London, invented the eraser in 1770. It was popularly called a "rubber" or "lead eater" because of the way "it wiped from the paper the marks of a black-lead pencil."

GRAPHITE PENCILS—The pencil was first described in 1565 by a Swissman, Konrad Gesner. He defined it as "a piece of lead in a stick of wood."

FOOD

CEREAL CRAZE—Cornflakes were first produced in 1898 by Will Kellogg of Battle Creek, Michigan. Today they are the most popular cereal in the world.

CHIP ACCIDENT—The first potato chips were really an accident! In 1853 an Indian chef, George Crum, was working at the Moon Lake House Hotel in Saratoga Springs. One day a diner asked him for thinner than normal French fried potatoes. They proved very popular and were known as "Saratoga chips."

DOUGHNUT SURPRISE—Believe it or not, the first doughnuts with holes were made in 1847 by a 15-year-old apprentice baker, Hanson Crocket, who was working in Camden, Maine. One morning he spotted uncooked dough in the center of his fried cakes, so he cut out the middle and produced the first ring doughnuts.

LEMONADE ICE POP—On a very cold night in 1905, Frank Epperson of San Francisco left a mixing stick in a glass of lemonade on his windowsill. In the morning the lemonade had frozen into the first ice pop.

HAMBURGER HUNGER—The first hamburgers were eaten by the Tartars, a Mongol people, in about 1240. Their recipe for a hamburger was raw, shredded camel, goat, or horsemeat made into a pâté.

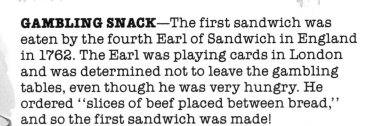

GAMBLING SNACK—The first sandwich was eaten by the fourth Earl of Sandwich in England in 1762. The Earl was playing cards in London and was determined not to leave the gambling tables, even though he was very hungry. He ordered ''slices of beef placed between bread,'' and so the first sandwich was made!

ICE CREAM DELIGHT—In the 17th century a French chef, Gerald Tissain, prepared the first ice cream. Charles I, who was king of England at that time, was so pleased that he paid the chef £20 (about $30) each year for the rest of his life.

PEANUT BUTTER DIET— If you like peanut butter you should thank a doctor from St. Louis. Trying to improve the diets of his patients, the doctor spread mashed peanuts on bread —a nutritious food that wasn't expensive.

DRINKS

MAGIC BERRIES—Legend tells us that around AD 850 an Abyssinian goatherd named Kaldi was very curious about the antics of his goats. They became very lively after eating the berries of an evergreen coffee bush. Kaldi decided to try some himself and found that they made him feel full of life. He met a Moslem monk who was always dozing off during prayers, so Kaldi gave him some of the berries, which kept the monk awake without any problem!

COFFEE CURE—Coffee served as a drink was first recorded around AD 1000 by the Arabian philosopher and physician, Aricenna.

For centuries coffee was mainly used as a medicine. It was only in the 16th century that it was drunk socially—in Arabia and Persia.

BRAIN BEVERAGE—Coca-Cola was invented by Dr. John Pemberton from Georgia. It was launched as a "brain tonic" in March 1886 and was first bottled in 1894 by Joseph Biedenham.

CURE FOR INDIGESTION—Pepsi-Cola was first made by the owner of a drugstore, Caleb Bradham of North Carolina, in 1898. It was devised to cure indigestion (dyspepsia), hence its name, "Pepsi."

HOT CHOCOLATE BEAN—
Cocoa was first prepared in
a powder form by Coenraad
van Houten of Holland in
1828. Cocoa butter was
extracted from the crushed
cacao bean.

HOLY DRINK—Whisky is
attributed to St. Patrick who
lived in Ireland in AD 450.
　Scotch whisky was first
distilled much later, in
1495, by Friar John Corr.
　Bourbon whisky was first
distilled from corn in 1789
by Rev. Elijah Craig from
Bourbon County, Kentucky.

DAIRY RECORD—Milk was
first sold in bottles in 1879
by the Echo Farm Dairy
Company of New York.

BENEDICTINE NECTAR—
Champagne was first produced in
1688 by Dom Pierre Perignon. He
was a monk in charge of the cellar
at the Benedictine Abbey of
Hautvilliers in Champagne, France.

TEA TALE—Tea was first
introduced into Europe from
Southeast Asia by the Dutch
East India Company in 1609.
　It was not until 1826 that
tea was first sold in packets
—this was on the Isle of
Wight in England by John
Horniman. The first tea bags
were produced by Joseph
Krieger from San Francisco
in 1920.

TOOLS

EARLY WRENCHES—The history of wrenches is not clear, but various types were made in Italy and France to turn nuts and bolts from about 1550 onward. Wrenches with movable jaws date from about 1700 and are sometimes known as "French wrenches."

POMPEII TOOLS—In AD 79 the Romans used planes for smoothing wood. Examples of planes have been found among the ruins of Pompeii.

The first metal plane was made in 1880 by Leonard Bailey of Boston.

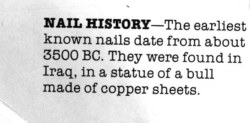

NAIL HISTORY—The earliest known nails date from about 3500 BC. They were found in Iraq, in a statue of a bull made of copper sheets.

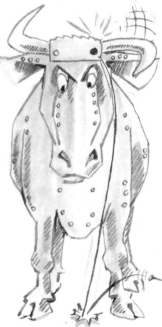

SAW SUCCESS—The saw is one of the earliest known tools. In 3000 BC Egyptians were using saws to cut wood and stone. Saw marks can be seen on the stone of the Pyramids.

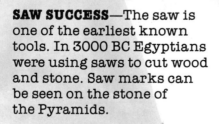

WHEELBARROW WONDER—
Believe it or not, the first wheelbarrow was thought to have been in use in China as early as AD 100.

GUN GADGET—Screws were a development from the nail and first appeared in the 16th century. In about 1550 screwdrivers were known as "turnscrews" and were used by gunsmiths to adjust their gun mechanisms.

WHEEL REPAIRER—In about 1250 V. de Honnecourt of France illustrated the screw jack. It is a hand-operated tool and can lift and support great weights with little human effort. In the 16th century the screw jack was widely used in Germany and Holland to lift up fully loaded wagons and so repair damaged wheels.

FIRST LAWNMOWER—The lawnmower was invented by Edwin Budding of Gloucester, England. In 1830 he signed an agreement with John Ferrabee of the Phoenix Iron Works in England for the manufacture of "machinery for . . . shearing the vegetable surface of lawns."

RICHES FROM THE EARTH

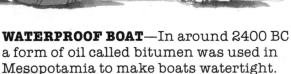

LAMP LIGHTER—
The first use of natural gas was for lighting 30 street lamps in Fredonia, New York, in 1821.

WATERPROOF BOAT—In around 2400 BC a form of oil called bitumen was used in Mesopotamia to make boats watertight.

SILVER FIND—Silver was one of the earliest metals ever used. Silver ornaments have been found in the royal tombs in Egypt dating as far back as 4000 BC.

In 1903 Fred La Rose, a blacksmith from Ontario, threw his hammer at a roaming fox and quite by chance struck silver. The hammer landed on what turned out to be the richest vein of silver ever. He sold his claim for $30,000 and by 1913 the vein had yielded silver worth $300 million!

DIAMOND RING—Diamonds are the earth's hardest known natural substance. They were first recorded in India in about 300 BC.

The first diamond engagement ring was made in 1477 for Archduke Maximilian, the 18-year-old son of the Holy Roman Emperor, Frederick III. Diamonds were set in a gold ring in the shape of ''M,'' for Mary, his future bride.

GOLD RIVERS—Gold is one of the most precious metals and was first known in the Middle East about 4000 BC. The earliest gold was obtained from riverbeds. During Roman times, gold mines as deep as 250 feet were in production in Spain.

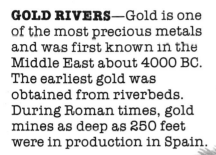

SOLID FUEL—Coal was first dug up around 2000 BC in Europe. In AD 100, it was used as a fuel by the Romans in northern Europe.

RADIUM DISCOVERY—Radium is a very rare, shining-white metal that is radioactive. It was discovered in 1898 by Pierre and Marie Curie of France.

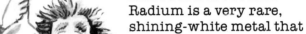

COPPER ISLAND—It is believed that copper was known before 4000 BC and was the first metal ever used. The earliest evidence of copper working was a smelting site in Yugoslavia.

Copper takes its name from the Mediterranean island of Cyprus.

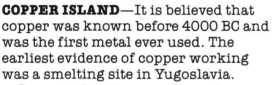

WROUGHT IRON—The Hittites, of Anatolia in Turkey, first produced wrought iron about 1500 BC. They burned the iron ore, which was dug from the ground, and made it as pure as possible by hammering.

NEW MATERIALS

CLAY CITY—The oldest known bricks were used to build the city of Jericho, Jordan, in about 6000 BC. The bricks were made from clay, reinforced with straw, and baked in the sun.

The first brick-making machine was built in 1839 by Cooke and Cunningham of Great Britain. The machine could make as many as 18,000 bricks in 10 hours.

CONCRETE TEMPLE—The first known use of concrete was in the lining of an aqueduct. The aqueduct was built about 700 BC in Jerwan, Iraq.

The first concrete building was the Temple of Concord, built in 121 BC in Rome.

GLASS FIRST—Glass was first made in 3000 BC in the Middle East by melting together sand and soda ash. By the first century BC, Syrians were using blowpipes to make glass vessels, but it was over 1,000 years before flat glass was first in use. It appeared in Europe around AD 1300.

ROOF-TOP INVENTION—The earliest known roof tiles were from the Temple of Heva at Olympia, Greece. The tiles were made of clay and date from 640 BC.

SILK SUBSTITUTE—Rayon was the first artificial fiber. It was produced by Hilaire de Chardonnet of France in 1884. Rayon is made from plant cellulose and is called "rayon" because of its shine. It is often used as imitation silk.

NYLON NEWS—Nylon was first made by W. Carothers and was patented in 1935. It is made from a coal tar chemical called benzene. The first product in which nylon was used was the toothbrush.

ANCIENT PAINTINGS—The first evidence of paint was in cave paintings in France, dating from about 25,000 BC. Pigments such as iron and manganese oxides were used to give yellow, red, and black colors.

33

INSTRUMENTS FOR MEASURING

EGYPTIAN MEASUREMENT—
About 3000 BC the Egyptians used the "cubit"—a measurement of about 18 in. It was the distance from the elbow to the tip of the middle finger.

METRIC MEASUREMENT—
In 1793 the French National Assembly began the metric system. The meter was defined as one ten-millionth of the distance from the North Pole to the Equator.

ITALIAN INVENTION—
In Italy in 1593 Galileo Galilei designed a thermoscope to measure the temperature of the air.

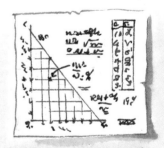

CLOCK FIRST—The Egyptians were the first people to use a device for measuring time. As early as 2000 BC they were using a shadow clock.

ASTRONOMER'S IDEA—
In 1842 a Swedish astronomer, Anders Celsius, introduced the centigrade scale for measuring temperature.

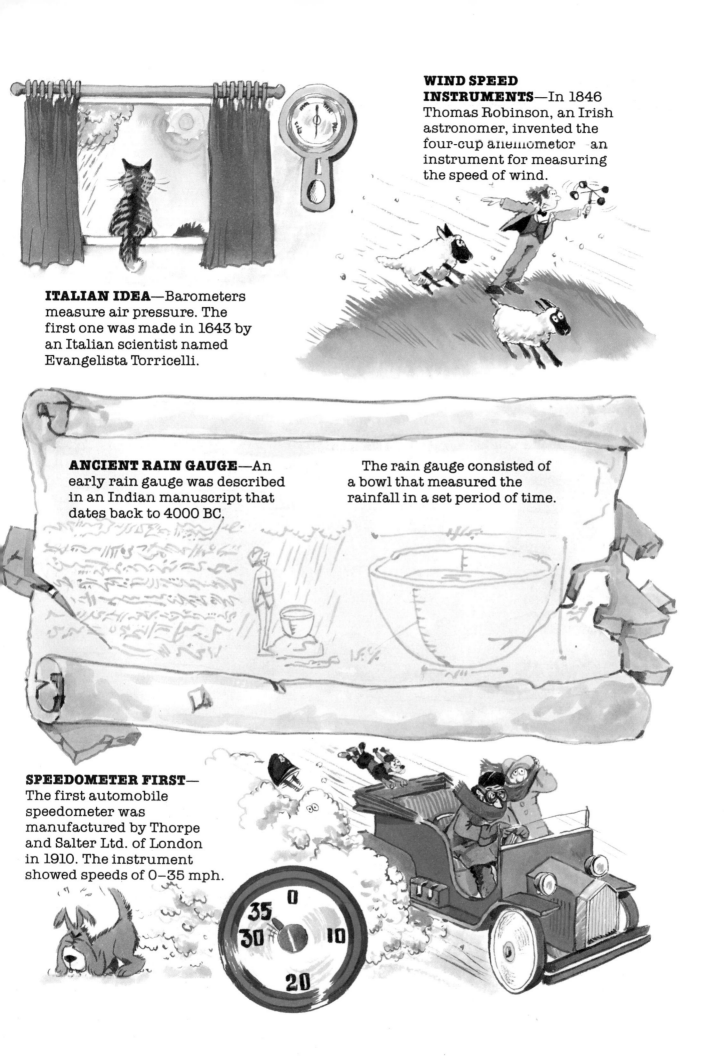

WIND SPEED INSTRUMENTS—In 1846 Thomas Robinson, an Irish astronomer, invented the four-cup anemometer—an instrument for measuring the speed of wind.

ITALIAN IDEA—Barometers measure air pressure. The first one was made in 1643 by an Italian scientist named Evangelista Torricelli.

ANCIENT RAIN GAUGE—An early rain gauge was described in an Indian manuscript that dates back to 4000 BC.

The rain gauge consisted of a bowl that measured the rainfall in a set period of time.

SPEEDOMETER FIRST—The first automobile speedometer was manufactured by Thorpe and Salter Ltd. of London in 1910. The instrument showed speeds of 0–35 mph.

MACHINES

TELE-MOLE TUNNELER—The first tunneling machine was devised in 1818 by Isambard Brunel. He designed the first machine for tunneling under the Thames River in England.

The first fully automatic tunneling machine, called the "Tele-Mole," was developed in the 1970s in Japan. It is controlled from the surface by an operator who keeps it on course with a laser beam that can be seen on a T.V. screen.

MIXING MACHINE—The first concrete mixer was used in 1857 for building a bridge over the Tisza River in Hungary.

STEAM ENGINE CONVERSION—In 1923 Benjamin Holt invented the first bulldozer. He fitted caterpillar tracks to a steam traction engine and attached a special blade to the front of the machine.

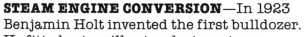

SNOWSTORM INVENTION—The first snowplow for clearing railroad tracks was built in 1883 by Leslie Brothers of Orangeville, Ontario. It was first used by the Canadian Pacific Railway.

ARCHITECT'S IDEA—In 10 BC a Roman architect named Vitruvius described a crane in his handbook for architects. The crane had a pulley at the top, which was held in position by ropes.

LAZY SHOPPER'S SOLUTION—In 1857 the Otis Steam Elevator Company in the United States installed the first passenger elevator. It was installed in a store in New York City and carried about six people. This invention encouraged the building of skyscrapers.

NOVELTY RIDE—The first escalator was designed by Jesse Reno in 1894 and was installed as a novelty ride on Coney Island Pier in New York. Today escalators are widely used in department stores, shopping malls, and airports.

ROADS, BRIDGES, AND CANALS

FIRST ROADS—The Romans began building the first paved roads throughout their empire in about 350 BC. For materials they used stone slabs on top of smaller stones set in mortar. The surface of the road was slightly curved to allow water to drain away on the sides.

ROMAN BRIDGE—The first stone bridge was built in 142 BC by Roman engineers. It spanned the Tiber River in Rome.

BOLTLESS BRIDGE—The first cast-iron bridge was built in 1779 by Abraham Darby and John Wilkinson. It stretches across the Severn River in England. Believe it or not, not one screw, rivet, nut, or bolt was used. The bridge is held together only by perfect dovetail joints.

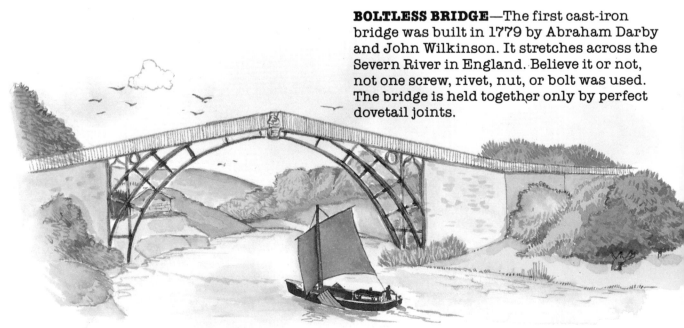

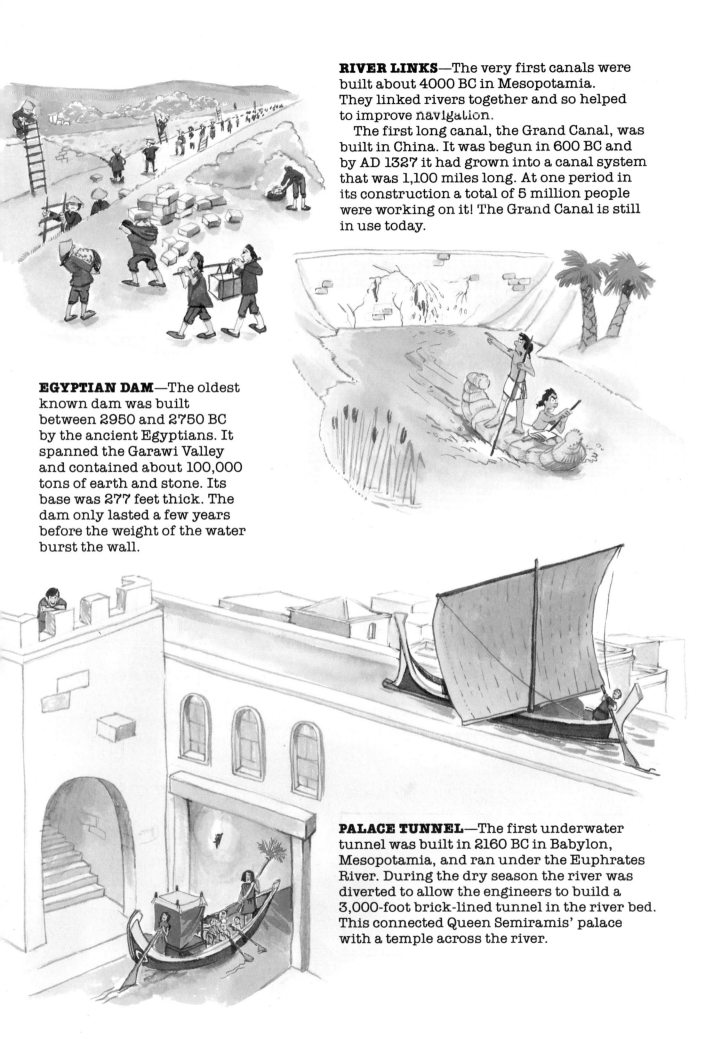

RIVER LINKS—The very first canals were built about 4000 BC in Mesopotamia. They linked rivers together and so helped to improve navigation.

The first long canal, the Grand Canal, was built in China. It was begun in 600 BC and by AD 1327 it had grown into a canal system that was 1,100 miles long. At one period in its construction a total of 5 million people were working on it! The Grand Canal is still in use today.

EGYPTIAN DAM—The oldest known dam was built between 2950 and 2750 BC by the ancient Egyptians. It spanned the Garawi Valley and contained about 100,000 tons of earth and stone. Its base was 277 feet thick. The dam only lasted a few years before the weight of the water burst the wall.

PALACE TUNNEL—The first underwater tunnel was built in 2160 BC in Babylon, Mesopotamia, and ran under the Euphrates River. During the dry season the river was diverted to allow the engineers to build a 3,000-foot brick-lined tunnel in the river bed. This connected Queen Semiramis' palace with a temple across the river.

BUILDINGS

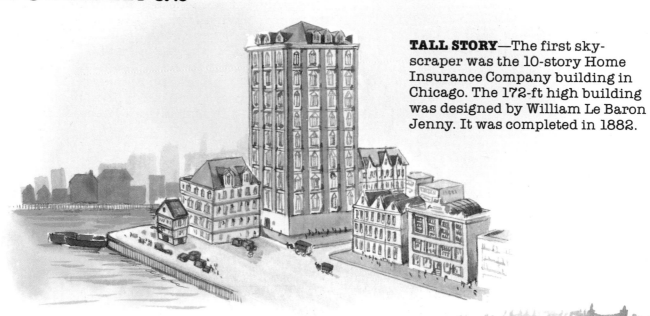

TALL STORY—The first sky-scraper was the 10-story Home Insurance Company building in Chicago. The 172-ft high building was designed by William Le Baron Jenny. It was completed in 1882.

GOOD FOOD—Low's Grand Hotel in London was the first hotel. It opened in 1774 and soon became known for its high-quality food.

SUPERMARKET STARTER—Michael Cullen of the United States started the first supermarket, on Long Island. It opened in 1930 and was known as ''King Kullen Food Stores.''

SHOPPING PALACE—The Marble Dry Goods Palace on Broadway in New York City was the first department store.

It was opened by Alexander Turney Stewart in 1848 and, at that time, was the largest store in the world!

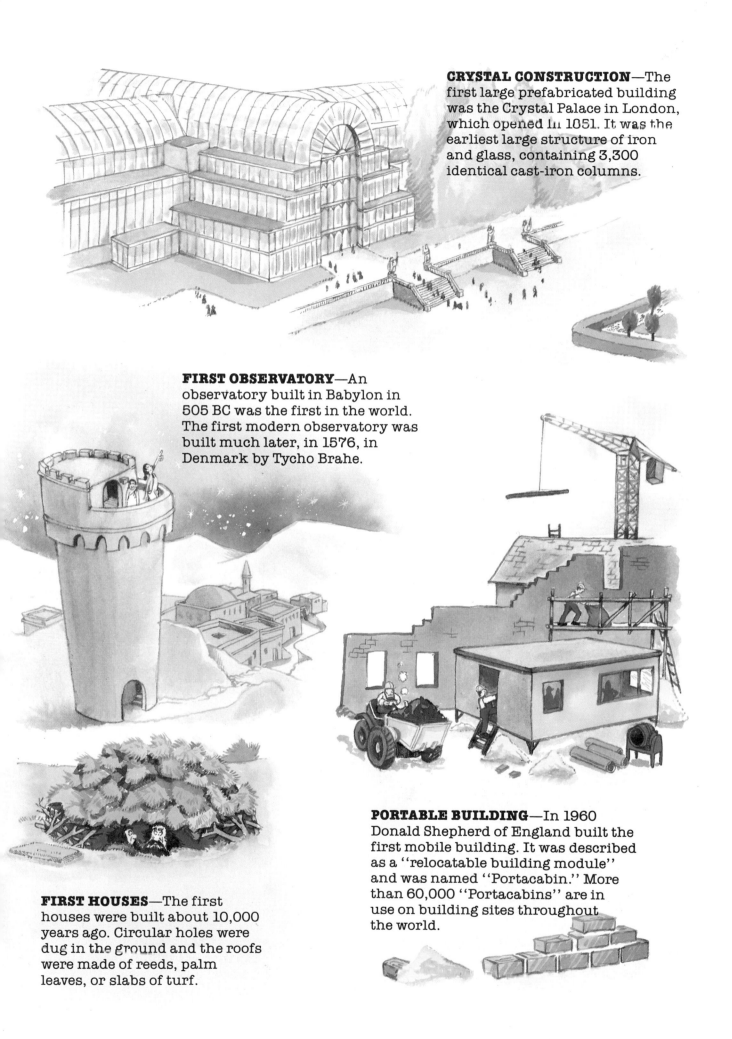

CRYSTAL CONSTRUCTION—The first large prefabricated building was the Crystal Palace in London, which opened in 1851. It was the earliest large structure of iron and glass, containing 3,300 identical cast-iron columns.

FIRST OBSERVATORY—An observatory built in Babylon in 505 BC was the first in the world. The first modern observatory was built much later, in 1576, in Denmark by Tycho Brahe.

PORTABLE BUILDING—In 1960 Donald Shepherd of England built the first mobile building. It was described as a "relocatable building module" and was named "Portacabin." More than 60,000 "Portacabins" are in use on building sites throughout the world.

FIRST HOUSES—The first houses were built about 10,000 years ago. Circular holes were dug in the ground and the roofs were made of reeds, palm leaves, or slabs of turf.

SAFETY

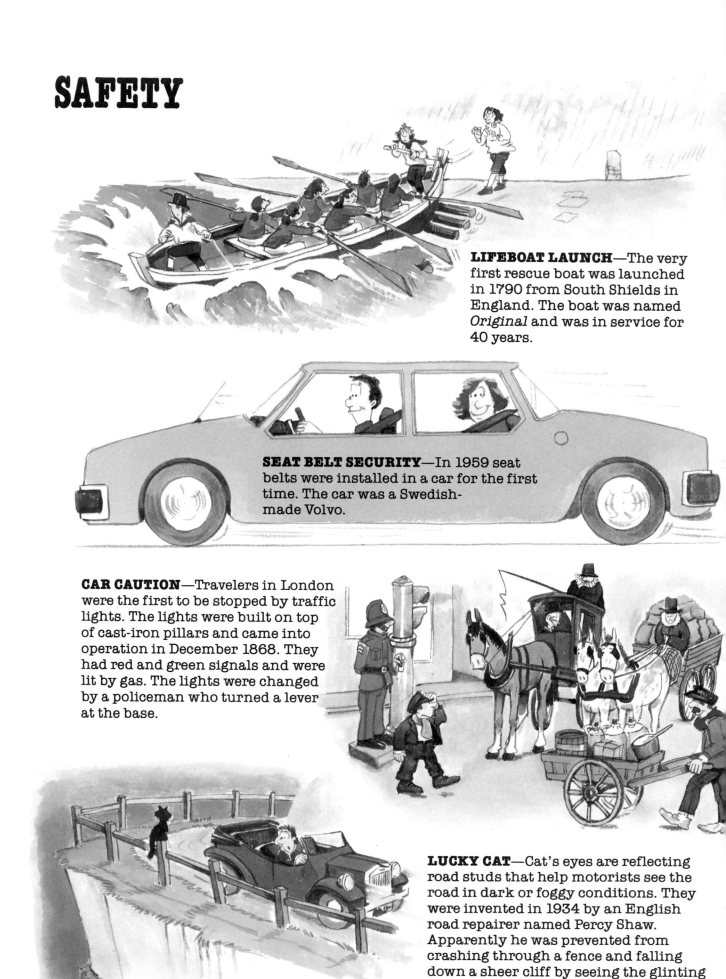

LIFEBOAT LAUNCH—The very first rescue boat was launched in 1790 from South Shields in England. The boat was named *Original* and was in service for 40 years.

SEAT BELT SECURITY—In 1959 seat belts were installed in a car for the first time. The car was a Swedish-made Volvo.

CAR CAUTION—Travelers in London were the first to be stopped by traffic lights. The lights were built on top of cast-iron pillars and came into operation in December 1868. They had red and green signals and were lit by gas. The lights were changed by a policeman who turned a lever at the base.

LUCKY CAT—Cat's eyes are reflecting road studs that help motorists see the road in dark or foggy conditions. They were invented in 1934 by an English road repairer named Percy Shaw. Apparently he was prevented from crashing through a fence and falling down a sheer cliff by seeing the glinting eyes of a cat sitting on a fence.

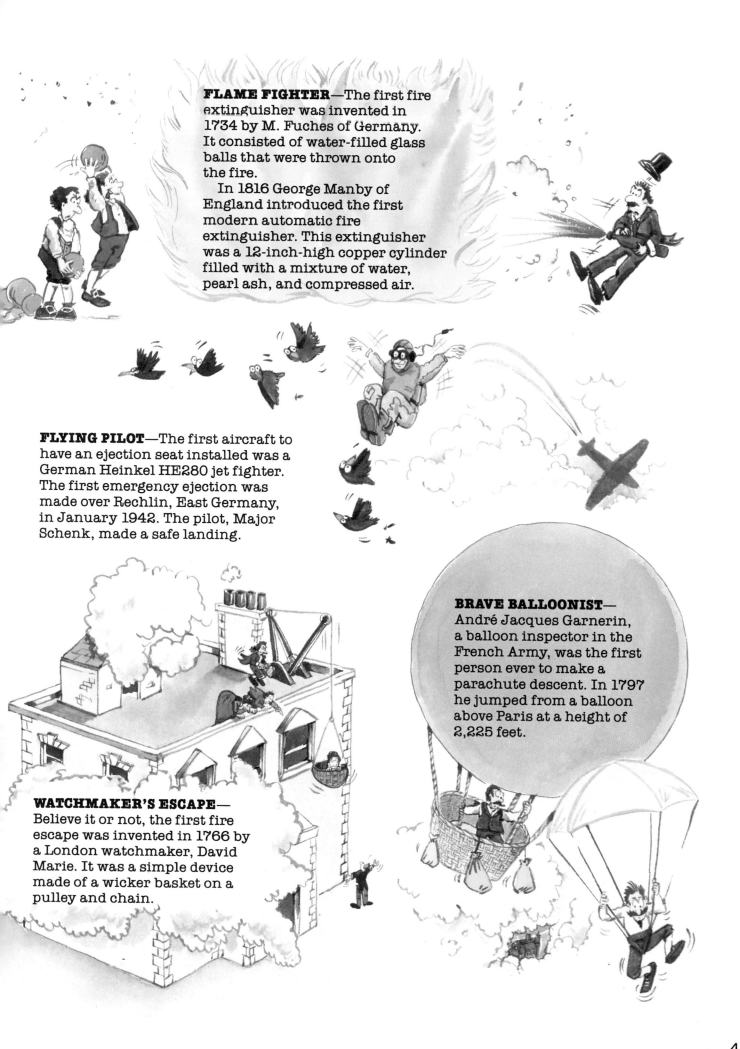

FLAME FIGHTER—The first fire extinguisher was invented in 1734 by M. Fuches of Germany. It consisted of water-filled glass balls that were thrown onto the fire.

In 1816 George Manby of England introduced the first modern automatic fire extinguisher. This extinguisher was a 12-inch-high copper cylinder filled with a mixture of water, pearl ash, and compressed air.

FLYING PILOT—The first aircraft to have an ejection seat installed was a German Heinkel HE280 jet fighter. The first emergency ejection was made over Rechlin, East Germany, in January 1942. The pilot, Major Schenk, made a safe landing.

WATCHMAKER'S ESCAPE—Believe it or not, the first fire escape was invented in 1766 by a London watchmaker, David Marie. It was a simple device made of a wicker basket on a pulley and chain.

BRAVE BALLOONIST—André Jacques Garnerin, a balloon inspector in the French Army, was the first person ever to make a parachute descent. In 1797 he jumped from a balloon above Paris at a height of 2,225 feet.

POWER AND ENERGY

FACTORY FIRST—The first tidal power station was called the Usine Marémotrice de la Rance and was opened in 1968 in France on the Rance River. The station took 5 years to build and now produces 544 million kilowatts of electricity each year.

SOLAR ENERGY—The simplest way to tap the sun's power is to collect its heat. In the 18th century Horace-Bénédict de Saussure, a Swiss scientist, designed the first solar heating panel. The panel reached a temperature of up to 190°F, enough to heat a bowl of soup.

NUCLEAR-POWERED TOWN—The first nuclear power station was built at Obninsk, USSR, and began producing electricity in 1954. It supplied enough electricity for a town of 6,000 people.

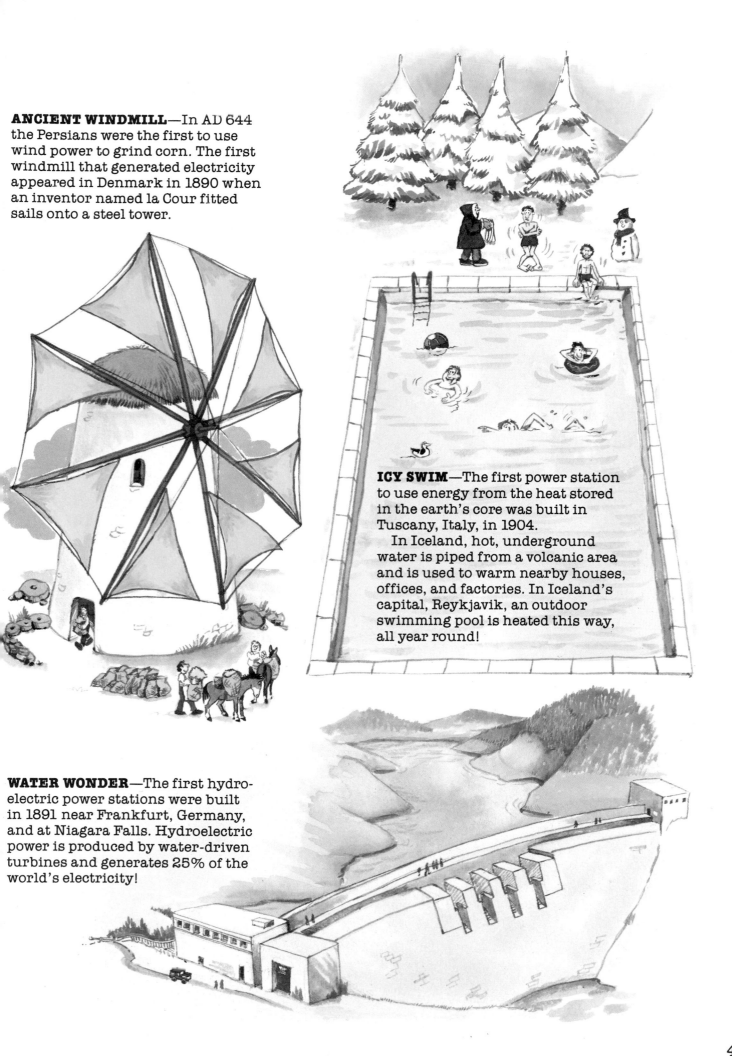

ANCIENT WINDMILL—In AD 644 the Persians were the first to use wind power to grind corn. The first windmill that generated electricity appeared in Denmark in 1890 when an inventor named la Cour fitted sails onto a steel tower.

ICY SWIM—The first power station to use energy from the heat stored in the earth's core was built in Tuscany, Italy, in 1904.

In Iceland, hot, underground water is piped from a volcanic area and is used to warm nearby houses, offices, and factories. In Iceland's capital, Reykjavik, an outdoor swimming pool is heated this way, all year round!

WATER WONDER—The first hydroelectric power stations were built in 1891 near Frankfurt, Germany, and at Niagara Falls. Hydroelectric power is produced by water-driven turbines and generates 25% of the world's electricity!

45

COMMUNICATIONS

CRYPTIC CODE—Morse code was introduced in 1838 by Samuel Morse of the United States. The code uses signals, transmitted electronically, consisting of patterns of short dots and long dashes that indicate numerals and the letters of the alphabet.

LONG-DISTANCE LINE—The first telephone was displayed to the public in Philadelphia in 1876. It was patented by Alexander Graham Bell, a Scottish-born inventor, and it contained the first microphone.

In 1884 the Bell Telephone Company of the United States set up the first ever long-distance telephone line—between Boston and New York. The year 1927 saw the first transatlantic telephone links—between New York and London.

TRANSATLANTIC TELEVISION—The first transatlantic live T.V. satellite transmission was via Telestar between Andover, Maine, and Goonhilly Downs, England, in 1962.

MOON TRANSMISSION—By 1965 a total of 300 million viewers in 9 countries were able to watch T.V. programs via the Early Bird satellite. A year later Luna 9, an unmanned space probe, landed on the moon and sent T.V. pictures back to earth.

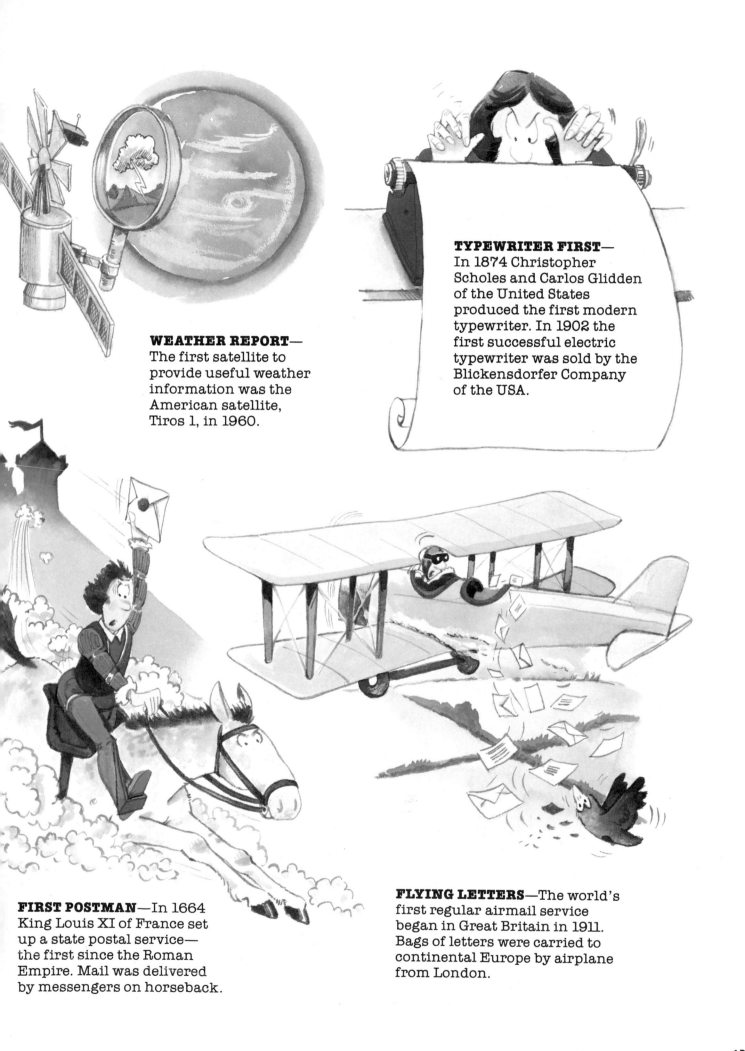

WEATHER REPORT—
The first satellite to
provide useful weather
information was the
American satellite,
Tiros 1, in 1960.

TYPEWRITER FIRST—
In 1874 Christopher
Scholes and Carlos Glidden
of the United States
produced the first modern
typewriter. In 1902 the
first successful electric
typewriter was sold by the
Blickensdorfer Company
of the USA.

FIRST POSTMAN—In 1664
King Louis XI of France set
up a state postal service—
the first since the Roman
Empire. Mail was delivered
by messengers on horseback.

FLYING LETTERS—The world's
first regular airmail service
began in Great Britain in 1911.
Bags of letters were carried to
continental Europe by airplane
from London.

HI-TECH

GIANT CALCULATOR—In 1945 Presper Eckert and John Maunchly of the United States designed the first fully-electronic computer. It was more like a giant calculator than a computer because it could not store data or programs.

COMPACT CAMERA—The first photographic camera was invented by Louis Daguerre and marketed by Alphonse Giroux of Paris in 1839.

In 1925 a German company, Leitz, designed one of the first small hand-held cameras.

LASER FIRST—In 1960 Theodore Maiman of the United States built a machine to make the first laser beams. Today, lasers are used for many different purposes, from surgical operations to cutting cloth.

3-D INVENTION—Holography is the technique of producing a three-dimensional photograph of an object by using laser beams. This was first demonstrated in 1963 by Emmett Leith and Juris Upatnieks of Michigan State University.

In 1984, *National Geographic* magazine was the first to show a hologram on its cover.

SPECTACULAR MICROSCOPE—In 1590 two Dutch eyeglass makers, Hans and Zacharias Janssen, made the first microscope. The lenses they used were not very powerful and therefore did not produce a very accurate image.

In 1683 Anton van Leeuwenhoek used a very powerful lens. This was so much more effective that, for the first time, bacteria could be seen. Not knowing what they were, van Leeuwenhoek described the bacteria as "little animals."

ATOMIC ACCURACY—In 1969 scientists in Washington D.C. built the first ammonia atomic clock. The clock is so accurate that it would take 1,700,000 years for it to be 1 second off!

GLASS TELEPHONE CABLE—In 1977 the General Telephone Co. of California introduced the first telephone fiber optic link. It enables thousands of telephone calls to be carried at the same time.

ROBOTS' WORK—The first industrial robots were made in the United States in 1962. They were "pick and place" robots, which are able to move an object from one place to another.

In the late 1970s robots began spot-welding and spray-painting cars. By 1983, the Yamazaki company of Japan was using robots to manufacture robots!

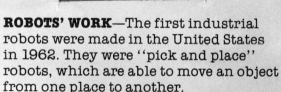

TINY RADIO—In 1985 Sony of Japan produced a miniature radio that was only one-tenth inch thick! It was nicknamed the "Credit Card Radio" because it was so thin.

MUSICAL INSTRUMENTS

EARLY IVORIES—The first piano was built in 1709 by Bartolomeo Cristofori of Florence, Italy. In 1800 John Hawkins of Philadelphia built the first upright piano.

ANCIENT STRINGS—The harp is the oldest instrument in the string section of the orchestra. It has been attributed to Jubal, son of Lamech and Adah (Genesis, Old Testament), at about 3875 BC.

MUSICAL COCONUT—The first ever reference to string instruments played with a bow appears in Persian and Chinese writings dating from about AD 800. The oldest known violin was an ancient instrument called a *kemantche*. It was played in Persia and consisted of a long stick that extended through half of a coconut.

PERCUSSION PIECE—The xylophone is said to have originated in Southeast Asia or Oceania. It was first mentioned in 1511 in Europe and was introduced into China from Burma at the end of the 18th century. The xylophone is one of the most important instruments in African music. It is also often used in the percussion section of an orchestra.

PREHISTORIC MUSIC—Bagpipes are a prehistoric Middle Eastern or Chinese instrument. They were originally made by shepherds, using lamb or goatskin.

PIPE PROGRESS—The recorder was originally developed from prehistoric pipes, although the first reference to them did not appear until 1388.

In 1690 J. C. Denner of Germany invented the first clarinet as a further development of the recorder.

JAZZ SOLO—In about 1840 a Belgian instrument maker named Antoine Joseph Sax patented the saxophone. It soon became a popular solo instrument and is widely used in jazz bands today.

SPANISH SERENADE—The guitar was developed from the ancient lute (a pear-shaped string instrument). It was brought to Europe by the Moors in the eighth century AD and became Spain's national instrument. It appeared in its present form about 1750.

TURKISH TUNES—Two percussion instruments, the cymbals and the triangle, were developed from Turkish military bands of ancient times. They were first used in an orchestra in 1680.

POTTERY DRUMS—Believe it or not, the first drums were made of pottery and were in the shape of an hourglass, with animal skins tied over both ends. Examples dating as far back as 4000 BC have been found in eastern Europe and along the Nile River.

MEDICINE

STETHOSCOPE FIRST—The first stethoscope was designed in 1816 by a Frenchman named René Laennec. Unlike the stethoscopes used today, it had only one earpiece. The modern ''two-ear'' stethoscope was designed in the United States in 1850.

ITALIAN INVENTION—In 1896 Dr. Riva-Rocci of Italy designed the first practical instrument for measuring blood pressure— the sphygmomanometer. Blood pressure that is too high or too low can affect a person's health.

X RAY DISCOVERY—Wilhelm Roentgen of West Germany was the first to discover X rays. X rays enable doctors to see inside a patient's body without having to perform surgery.

FIRST THERMOMETER—The first thermometer used for measuring body temperature was devised in 1625 by S. Santorino of Italy. The first clinical thermometer was introduced over 200 years later in 1863 by W. Aitkin of Great Britain.

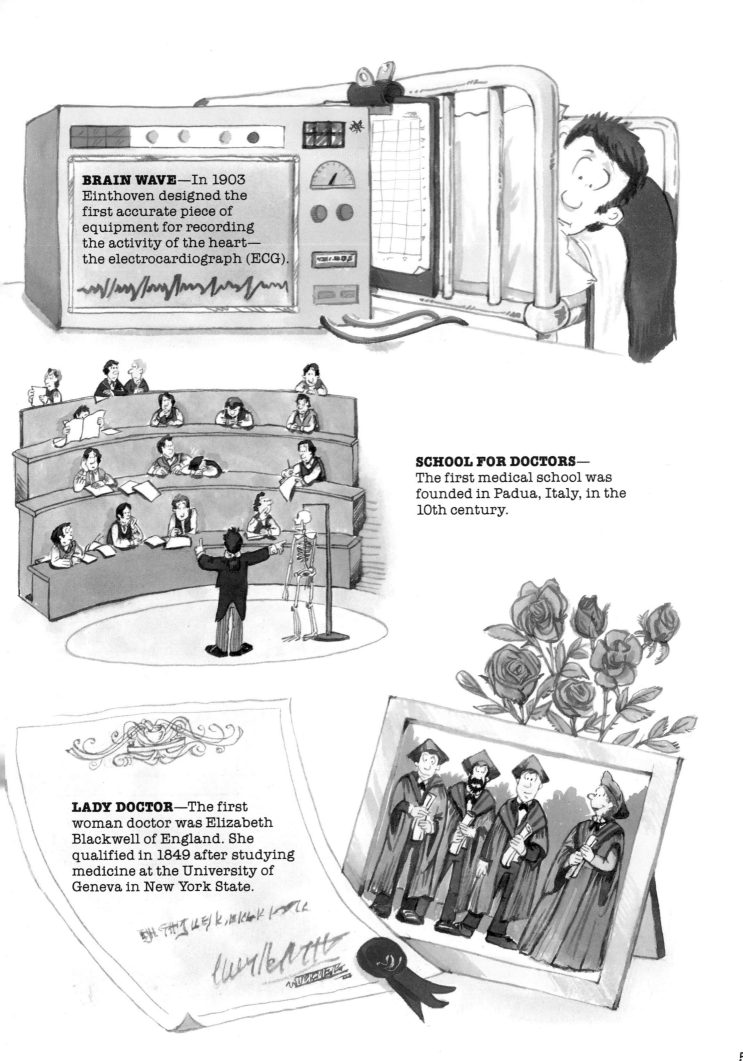

BRAIN WAVE—In 1903 Einthoven designed the first accurate piece of equipment for recording the activity of the heart—the electrocardiograph (ECG).

SCHOOL FOR DOCTORS—The first medical school was founded in Padua, Italy, in the 10th century.

LADY DOCTOR—The first woman doctor was Elizabeth Blackwell of England. She qualified in 1849 after studying medicine at the University of Geneva in New York State.

WHACKY INVENTIONS

BALLOON BIRDS—In 1887 Charles Wulff of Paris thought of an unusual design for a flying balloon. The power was to be supplied by large birds, such as eagles, which were to be tied to the framework of the machine.

PLANE CALAMITY—A Scottish engineer named Joseph Kaufmann patented his idea for an airplane in 1869. It consisted of a steam engine with wings that flapped like those of a bird. When he tried out a model of his extraordinary invention, the wings flapped so violently that the whole machine fell to pieces!

PADDLE INVENTION—In about 1850 an unnamed inventor built an "aqua cycle." The rider was supported on floats and used paddles attached to his feet to move forward. The machine was supposed to be used for duck hunting on lakes where the water was calm.

CLOCK SHOCK—George Hogan of Chicago designed a unique alarm clock. It awakened the sleeper by sending a stream of cold water down his or her neck!

EDIBLE RECORDS—A German company, Gebrüder Stollwerk, was granted a patent in 1903 for a phonograph that played flat discs made of chocolate wrapped in tinfoil. After the records had been played they could be eaten!

CHOCOLATE SPOON—In 1937 Constance Honey of London patented a chocolate spoon for giving bitter medicine to children!

MECHANICAL MAN—Perhaps one of the most unusual inventions was patented in 1868 by Zadoc Dederick and Isaac Grass of New Jersey. It was a partly-wheeled vehicle built in the form of a mechanical man pulling a cart. Powered by a steam engine built inside its body, the mechanical man was supposed to walk forward while pulling the vehicle behind him!

CRAZY CAR—In 1976 Charles William Clark of England patented a car powered by a giant rubber band!

SNOWBALL STORY—An Englishman named Arthur Paul Patrick came up with an amazing idea to water the Sahara Desert. His plan was to roll snowballs down a pipe from the North Pole. However, his scheme proved impractical, and the pipe was never built.

INDEX